AND ALL THAT IS U

A New Look at Women's Work

by ROSEMARY DAWSON

The report of the Industrial and Economic Affairs
Committee of the General Synod Board for
Social Responsibility

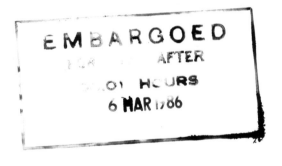

CHURCH HOUSE PUBLISHING
Church House, Gt Smith Street, London SW1P 3NZ

ISBN 0 7151 6568 2

Published 1986 for the General Synod Board for Social Responsibility by Church House Publishing

THIS REPORT
This report is offered as a contribution to debate because its contents are thought likely to prove of interest. It is not intended to represent the policy of the Board for Social Responsibility itself.

The Board is an advisory committee of the Church of England General Synod. Its functions are to promote and co-ordinate the thought and action of the Church in matters affecting the lives of men and women in society.

The Industrial and Economic Affairs Committee, which has commissioned this report, is a Constituent Committee of the Board. It has among its members and regular consultants: company directors, trade union officials, university lecturers, civil servants, bishops and industrial chaplains.

Cover design and photographs: Paul Skirrow.

Printed by Burgess & Son (Abingdon) Ltd

FOREWORD

by the Rt Rev. Simon Phipps, Bishop of Lincoln

And All That Is Unseen is a report commissioned by the Industrial and Economic Affairs Committee of the Board for Social Responsibility. It continues the Committee's tradition of producing documents on significant industrial and economic issues being faced by the nation. However, it differs from previous reports in this respect. It treats its subject matter specifically from a woman's point of view, and is written by a woman.

Its aim is to present a clear description of the facts about women's work, opportunities, expectations and roles, including a lucid section on the unseen and unpaid work in the home that most women do. It sets all this in the broad historical context, showing how industrialisation has changed the role of women in society. And in Part Two, it issues a challenge to the Churches to rethink our theology and reshape our practice, in the light of the evidence displayed in Part One.

The Gospels give us a number of stories of Jesus' relationship with women—representing them, using their ministry, engaging with them in serious conversation, making them as witnesses to his risen life. It is also often said that his example and teaching has resulted, over the centuries, in new attitudes to women and, at least potentially, in the freeing of women from certain prejudices and invalid traditions. In all this Jesus was not singling out women and women's interests over against those of men. His approach was, on the contrary, all of a piece with his way of seeing people as human beings and not in terms of gender. It was the woman's righting of an en-gendered imbalance. I hope that this essay will be read as a righting of the human imbalance, rather than as a grinding of any feminist axe.

I would like to thank the author, Rosemary Dawson, for this strenuous piece of work, and with her the members of the Working Group convened to oversee the project. My hope is that the essay will provide a basis for people in Church and society alike, in the rethinking of the place of women at work and at home, and in remaking the balance between women and men in a shared humanity.

SIMON LINCOLN
Chairman,
Industrial and Economic
Affairs Committee

CONTENTS

Part One

INTRODUCTION

Over the past few years one of the chief issues which the Church has sought
to address is the employment crisis. Many Christians, individually and
collectively, have been involved practically in efforts to lessen the pain of
unemployment by job creation schemes, drop-in centres, counselling and
political lobbying. Church boards and committees have produced reports
and discussion packs aimed at increasing the Church's awareness of and
involvement in employment issues. Along with others, Christians have been
asking wider questions about the nature and purpose of work, the
distribution of employment and wealth, and the impact of new technology.
They have recognised that considering these questions leads us to ask again
about the whole purpose of life, the nature of humanity and the being of
God.

Putting the Record Straight

The reason for writing this report is to further the discussion about working
life but to do it from an explicitly female viewpoint. This is usually a missing
dimension in reports on employment, reports which are almost always a
product of male groups and authors. There is a need to put the record
straight and balance the treatment of employment issues.

Part One aims to increase awareness of the facts and trends in female
employment in a concise way for those who do not have time to go rooting
through Department of Employment statistics. Against the argument that
now is not the time to debate the employment position of women (after all,
over $3\frac{1}{2}$ million people have no jobs at all), it is argued that the current
situation makes it all the more important that we discuss it now. Much
popular prejudice maintains that married women ought not to be in the
labour force at all when jobs are in such short supply. Economic recession
makes it dangerously easy to slide into sexism or racism. We are at a critical
juncture, and must resist the pressure on women to relinquish some of the
gains they have made on the road to equality by giving up their jobs to men.

1

Chapter One presents the facts about women's employment, looking particularly at recent general statistics and at part-time employment. In Chapters Two and Three, suggestions are made concerning why women occupy a secondary status within the labour market. The chief cause certainly appears to revolve around the issue of the role and responsibility of women for unpaid housework and childcare. Though not seen, quantified or rewarded, housework does constitute work. Therefore, as far as possible, 'work' will not be equated with 'paid employment' in this report. For women this is not their reality.

What is women's reality is that they undertake the vast task of unpaid work that needs to be done in our society, and that their paid work too is likely to be undervalued and invisible. We recognise, of course, that there is a great diversity of experience among employed women. A woman's experience of employment depends upon a number of interrelated factors —training, pay, domestic circumstances and others. Nevertheless it remains true that 'women's work' generally is something which does not often merit serious thought, something which many men are above doing or considering. It concerns private places and private lives, and its relation to what is public, paid and 'important' is ignored.

The sexual division of labour in our society has developed rapidly since the beginning of the Industrial Revolution, and so Chapter Four looks in particular at the effects of industrialisation on the role of women in society. The development of two distinct spheres—public and private—is examined, with some of its consequences for the Church's thinking and attitudes also being spelt out.

Part Two examines three particular areas for Christian thought and action, with an introduction in Chapter Five to the theological approach being adopted and the convictions that underlie it. Chapter Six considers Justice. That women have fewer chances for gainful employment, recognition and status, because they are women (and the evidence certainly points that way), is unjust and something about which the Church should be concerned. If a person is at an immediate disadvantage from birth, because she is female, and at a still greater one if also black, then the Church needs to be asking what it can do not simply to make the consequences of disadvantage easier to bear but to alter the situation by challenging the structures that cause that injustice.

In Chapter Seven, under the heading of Stewardship and Servanthood, we ask questions about the nature and purpose of work, and make a plea that women's definitions and experiences should be heard. The proper stewardship of resources concerns not only 'time and talents'. It concerns caring for dependents, educating children and meeting common human needs. These are often thought of as women's domain. But many men are now rediscovering the importance of this work.

However great the Church's commitment to exploring these areas, and however valuable its contributions, its achievements will be hollow if its own life and structures are left untouched. This is the subject matter for Chapter Eight. The Church needs to clarify its vision of the Kingdom of God and the reign of Justice. It needs to affirm the positive role of paid and unpaid work in people's lives. But the Church must first come to terms with and amend its own sexist practices and prejudices. Only then will it be truly fulfilling its God-given mission to enable women and men to have life, and to have it more abundantly.

The title of this Report 'And All that is Unseen' was chosen deliberately to highlight the invisibility of much of the work done by women. It is an indirect allusion to the Nicene Creed. God is 'Maker of all things, seen and unseen'. There is nothing which is outside of God's concern.

Chapter One

WOMEN AND WORK—SOME FACTS AND FIGURES

Male and female he created them. And God blessed them, and God said to them, 'Be fruitful and multiply, and fill the earth and subdue it, and have dominion over the fish of the sea and over the birds of the air and over every living thing that moves upon the earth'.[1]

Work has always been a way of life. People need to work in order to live. How work is allocated, structured and rewarded, however, is up to us. There is nothing inevitable about our present structuring of work. How we choose to do this will depend on our understanding of what work is for.

Work is not only for ensuring our physical survival. At its best it can be much more than that. It presents an opportunity for the development of our creative energies and talents. It locates us socially as part of a network of relationships and mutual obligations. It assures us of our value, of our ability to contribute to society. Work of some kind fulfils a variety of human needs and therefore is necessary for human wholeness.

If waging work is part of how we choose to structure and value it then it needs to be widely available—and to discriminate against women, ethnic groups or young people in its allocation is to place a lower value on their lives, because it is denying them a path to fulfilment. Clearly in our society paid employment is not available to all, nor is it likely to be in the foreseeable future. It is imperative therefore to seek ways to revalue and reorganise work so that everybody has access to it.

Current General Statistics on Women's Employment

The participation of women in the labour market is sometimes regarded as a fairly recent development. A luxury perhaps, which a prosperous society enjoying full employment can indulge, but which ought to be relinquished in view of the current economic crisis. It may come to some as a surprise to

4

learn that women have in fact made up nearly one-third of the labour force for more than a century. In 1850 when government statisticians first distinguished between women and men in their statistics, female employees accounted for 31 per cent of the labour force. This figure remained constant until 1951. It rose to 36 per cent in 1961 and to 40·2 per cent in 1981.[2]

In spite of a recent sharp increase in this the statistics show that there is nothing new about female employment. Few working class women have ever had the choice to stay at home rather than go out to work.

PROPORTIONS OF EMPLOYED WOMEN IN FULL-TIME & PART-TIME JOBS   GHS 1981

SINGLE WOMEN WITHOUT DEPENDENT CHILDREN.

13% PART TIME

87% FULL TIME

MARRIED WOMEN WITHOUT DEPENDENT CHILDREN

40% PART TIME

60% FULL TIME

WOMEN WITH DEPENDENT CHILDREN

69% PART TIME

31% FULL TIME

However, what is striking about the statistics is the increase in the numbers of married women in the labour force. Whereas one-tenth of married women were registered in the 1910 employment statistics, the figure was one-fifth in 1951. Now almost two-thirds of employed women are married, the economic activity rate of wives having trebled during the last 30 years. Ann Oakley[3] points out that if the participation of men in the labour market was also seen in relation to their marital status, it would become clear that the changes have occurred in marriage patterns as much as in employment.

More married men are employed too, because more people marry, marry earlier and live and work longer than they did a century ago. But other factors are also needed to account for the rise in women's participation in the labour market. Two world wars not only brought large numbers of women back into employment, but also into the 'male' occupations within it. Birth control and better health provision have meant that women spend a smaller proportion of their adult lives bearing and raising children, hence the greater demand for jobs.

The Department of Employment's Women and Employment Survey,[4] published in 1984, found that women now spend more of their adult lives in employment than ever before. Only 1 in 100 women aged between 45 and 55 have never had a paid job. The economic activity of women varies according to marital status, the number and ages of children, and the stage of life-cycle reached. The rates of economic activity (that is, the number of women available for employment) are highest among teenagers because few are yet mothers (88 per cent). Other than teenagers, women in their 40s have the highest economic activity rates (78 per cent). A woman's peak childbearing years are the mid-late 20s and this is reflected in the lower rates of economic activity for this age group (54 per cent). However, the proportion of women returning to employment is greatest among women of this age. The two-phase model—according to which the economic activity of women is interrupted by a long break of about seven years for bearing and raising children—is now less applicable as many women are returning to employment between the births of their children.

'Trend evidence suggests that more and more women will be attached to the labour market for most of their working lives' conclude the authors of the Department of Employment report. Consequently, employment cannot be regarded as something which is marginal to women's lives or to the lives of their families.[5]

Part-time Employment

While marriage in itself rarely determines whether or not women look for jobs it does affect the number of hours they work in them. The increase in married women's employment has been closely allied with the growth of part-time work which is particularly attractive to mothers of young children.

Britain has the highest proportion of part-time workers among its female workforce of any country in the Western world. 44 per cent are part-timers, that is 20 per cent of the total labour force. The 1981 Census revealed that of 21,148,000 employed people, 4,468,000 worked in part-time jobs and the University of Warwick's Institute for Employment Research[6] forecasts that this figure will continue to rise.

Between 1961 and 1971 full-time employment in manufacturing fell by 16 per cent but part-time jobs increased by 21 per cent.[7] However, the opportunities for part-time work exist predominantly in the service industries—in cleaning, selling and clerical work. The expansion of those industries between 1961 and 1971 created jobs for 1·2 million women, mostly part-time.[8] Much of the labour required by the service industries is more conveniently carried out on a part-time basis because it takes place outside of normal work hours (cleaning in offices for example). In manufacturing industries, evening shifts make for the more efficient use of equipment.

Disadvantages of Part-time Work

For many women part-time work is a long-term arrangement which allows them to combine employment with domestic duties. But there is a price to be paid. Despite the increase in the number of part-time jobs during the last 30 years there has been little improvement in the nature and conditions of such work. It is still overwhelmingly concentrated within low skilled occupations, characterised by low pay, lack of training opportunities and poor promotion prospects.

The need to be employed on a part-time basis means that many women are forced to take up occupations below the level at which they were previously engaged full-time.

One in 25 female part-time employees have a teaching qualification; 1 in 12 have a nursing qualification and 1 in 6 have received clerical training.

Career orientated women who wish to spend time out of full employment while they raise families find that their total career prospects suffer—and particularly if there are no part-time opportunities in their occupation.

Sara Holmes is a single parent of two children. In 1984 she appealed to an Industrial Tribunal for the right to work part-time in her civil service job. She won her case.[9] This breakthrough could encourage more women to seek the right to work part-time in well-paid, higher-status areas of work and raise the status of part-time employment. Job-sharing may also be a significant initiative, opening up opportunities for part-time employment in white collar and professional occupations.

Many people regard full-time employment as the only viable form of employment. They assume that 'part-timers' are less committed to their work, although 20 per cent of the labour force have part-time jobs. Though essential to the economy, part-time work is treated as secondary. This will not change until part-time workers have the same rights and benefits as full-time workers. Moves to redress this inequality have so far been unsuccessful. A draft directive by the European Commission requiring member states of the European community to grant 'part-timers' pro rata rights is being strongly resisted by the British government.[10]

Although, as we have seen, women constitute over 40 per cent of the labour force, prejudices persist against women in employment. These prejudices resurface in an alarming fashion at times of high unemployment. Behind the prejudices lies the conviction that the employment of men is a priority. This is particularly the case where women are married. But even when they are single and childless, support themselves financially and are able and ambitious, they still do not have the same opportunities.

Only 6 per cent of women interviewed in the Department of Employment survey[11] said that they would prefer not to go out to work. Women want employment for much the same reasons as men—for money, status, fulfilment and companionship.

Chapter Two

WOMEN AND WORK—THE ISSUES

Occupational Segregation

Newspaper headlines which sensationalise the breakthrough of women into previously all-male preserves create and reinforce the common belief that 'women have now got equal rights', and that all barriers to their equal participation in employment have been overcome. That Margaret Thatcher is Prime Minister is taken as proof that any woman can make it to the top if she tries. That more women are not at the top is taken as proof that women, after all, prefer home and hearth to the cut and thrust world of business, industry and politics.

In spite of well publicised exceptions—women in space and so forth—the vast majority of women are found working within a limited range of occupations and industries. Within the service industries they are mainly engaged in clerical, cleaning and catering work. Within manufacturing they are found predominantly in textiles and footwear, food, drink and tobacco, and light engineering. The visible increase in the numbers of employed women has not been matched by a corresponding increase in the variety of jobs that they do. Women are overwhelmingly engaged in low-status, low-paid and less-skilled jobs. 63 per cent of employed women work in segregated jobs in low-status occupations. 81 per cent of employed men work only with other men.[1] Occupational segregation operates on two planes. 'Vertical' segregation describes the situation where women and men have different jobs within an industry. 'Horizontal' segregation describes the situation where both sexes have the same type of job but one sex performs more skilled, responsible or senior work.

Commenting on the finding that 'the husband's world of work is more peopled by men than their wives' world of work by women' the authors of the Department of Employment survey suggested that 'this experience shapes men's attitude towards women's qualities as workers'.[2] If men do not work with women and only observe women doing unskilled work, it is not surprising that they develop prejudices about women's capabilities.

OCCUPATIONAL DISTRIBUTION AMONG FEMALE MANUAL & NON-MANUAL WORKERS

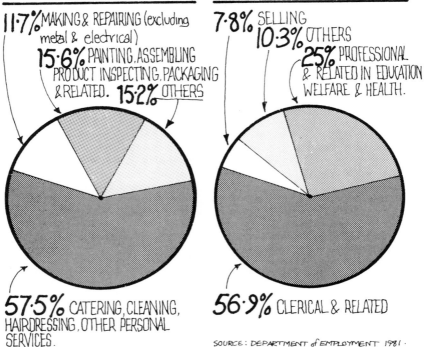

FEMALE MANUAL WORKERS · FEMALE NON-MANUAL WORKERS

11·7% MAKING & REPAIRING (excluding metal & electrical)

15·6% PAINTING, ASSEMBLING PRODUCT INSPECTING, PACKAGING & RELATED. 15·2% OTHERS

57·5% CATERING, CLEANING, HAIRDRESSING, OTHER PERSONAL SERVICES.

7·8% SELLING

10·3% OTHERS

25% PROFESSIONAL & RELATED IN EDUCATION WELFARE & HEALTH.

56·9% CLERICAL & RELATED

SOURCE: DEPARTMENT of EMPLOYMENT 1981.

Most professions, other than teaching and nursing, are heavily male dominated. Even within the 'female' professions, men occupy most of the senior and supervisory posts. For example, 80 per cent of primary school teachers are women, but 56.3 per cent of primary head teachers are men. Women make up 45 per cent of secondary teachers but account for only 16 per cent of secondary head teachers.[3] One per cent of civil engineers, judges and university professors are women. Two per cent of accountants, 3 per cent of Members of Parliament, 6 per cent of solicitors, 10 per cent of university lecturers and 13 per cent of managers are women.[4]

There are several possible reasons for the persistence of occupational segregation.

Attitudes

Old attitudes die hard. Outmoded and negative views about the nature and capabilities of 'working women' are one reason why it proves so difficult to break down the stereotypes of 'women's work' and 'men's work'.

Women are said to shun dirty work or to be physically unable to lift heavy loads. The steady trickle of women into the manual trades as plumbers, joiners and builders is challenging this myth. It is argued that women do not have the necessary characteristics and qualities to get on in a man's world. They are too emotional, irrational and unreliable, too pushy or not ambitious enough. There is also the belief that children require the full-time attention of their mothers.

Possibly such doubts about the ability of women reflect in part the inability of men to face the prospect of female competition. Perhaps they disguise men's fears for both job security and the comforts of home life.

Sex Stereotyping

Children are still brought up very differently according to whether they are girls or boys, and encouraged to develop the characteristics, preferences and aptitudes deemed appropriate to their sex. Even in the 1980s, parents often place less emphasis upon the need of girls for education and training than they do of boys. Girls are raised with the expectation that a job is a prelude to the main purpose and business of living, which is to raise a family of their own, and they are not encouraged to look beyond their child-rearing years to other areas of interest or employment.

Such conditioning can be pervasive enough to close options off to girls (and boys) early on in their lives.

The Equal Opportunities Commission has done valuable work in promoting awareness of sex stereotyping and of how early in life it occurs. Through its extensive range of publications it has helped to promote the work which is now going on in many schools to encourage girls and boys to take up courses in non-traditional subjects. To be successful in preventing sex stereotyping, schools need to work both on the structure of the curriculum and on the presentation and content of courses. This is pointed out in the Commission's publication 'Do you Provide Equal Educational Opportunities?':

> The opportunities which pupils are given to study non-traditional subjects should be real opportunities and not token gestures. While many schools offer an

apparent choice, the grouping of the subjects and the time-tabling arrangements can discourage pupils from selecting a subject which is non-traditional. It is also important to ensure that the structural alterations in a school which allow pupils to have access to non-traditional subjects are accompanied by a reconstruction of the curriculum content, so that the objects are interesting and attractive for both sexes. For example, boys may be more attracted to home economics if the programme includes making denim jackets or cord trousers (or whatever is the latest fashion), painting and decorating, etc. Similarly, metalwork could include jewellery making, wrought iron work, etc, and traditional courses for girls such as office studies should be extended to incorporate business management skills and accountancy as well as shorthand and typing. These curriculum developments can be supported by inviting adults to talk to the pupils about their work in non-traditional roles.[5]

Training

Another important reason why women are concentrated in low paid, semi-skilled work is that training opportunities are extended more readily to boys than to girls. Girls receive less training in their first jobs than do boys and the length of the training they receive is shorter. Figures showing the numbers of employees released by their employers to take non-advanced courses at major establishments of Further Education expose this imbalance. Of the 313,000 people released in 1982, 80 per cent were male.[6] Women constitute a small minority of apprentices numbering 3,900 out of a total 123,700,[7] and their apprenticeships are likely to be in the traditionally 'feminine' areas of hairdressing and catering. The training that girls are receiving is not challenging the assumptions about male and female roles. 72 per cent of people completing a Manpower Services Commission (MSC) Training Opportunities Programme (TOPS) course in food preparation and serving were women. But only 8 per cent of people completing the TOPS Science and Technology course were women, and on the welding and construction course the figure was 0·5 per cent. Other MSC schemes have been criticised for perpetuating sex stereotypes, such as the Information Technology Centres (ITEC) in which girl participants make up only 26 per cent of the total.

Women and Low Pay

One-third of the workforce in this country, about 7 million adults, receive less than two-thirds of the average male manual worker's wage. This is the Trades Union Congress (TUC) definition of low pay which stands at £2·70 an hour or £105 a week in 1984/5. This section looks at the position of low paid women workers. Why are so many women low paid? What has the effect of the Equal Pay Act been? And what are the consequences for families?

12

WOMEN'S AVERAGE GROSS HOURLY EARNINGS AS A PROPORTION OF MEN'S, EXCLUDING THE EFFECTS OF OVERTIME, FULL-TIME EMPLOYEES AGED 18 & OVER 1970 83

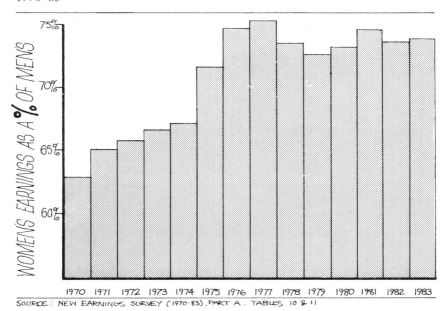

SOURCE: NEW EARNINGS SURVEY (1970·83). PART A. TABLES 10 & 11

Low pay is very much a 'women's issue'. Two-thirds of all low paid full-time employees are women. 15 per cent of full-time male employees are low paid in comparison with 52 per cent of full-time female employees. Among people working part-time the proportion, is of course, much higher.

The Department of Employment's survey of earnings[8] gave details of the ten lowest paid jobs—all of them traditionally women's. Hairdressers fared worst, earning £74·50 a week; waitresses earned £78·00 and saleswomen £80·20. The lowest paid male occupational group were hospital porters. They earned a weekly average of £83·45, excluding overtime and shift premium. The large wage differentials between even the lowest paid of women and men cannot be ignored.

The persistence of low pay among women workers reflects in part the failure of the 1970 Equal Pay Act which aimed to redress wage inequalities between women and men. The Act had a short-term effect in narrowing differentials, but New Earnings Survey (NES) statistics show that the gap is widening again.[9] In 1977 women's earnings reached a peak of 75·5 per cent of men's, but progress halted here as the initial effects of the legislation worked through and the effects of the recession began to be felt. By 1983 women's earnings were 73·3 per cent of men's.

The failure of the act was due in large measure to its limited aims. It did not take the nature of women's employment sufficiently into account. The highest concentration of low paid workers is to be found in those industries in which women predominate—the clothing industry, retailing, hairdressing, and hotel and catering. The Equal Pay Act stipulated that women and men must receive equal remuneration if their work was 'of the same or a broadly similar nature'. Therefore, for a woman to claim equal pay, there had to be a man on the same job at the same workplace. The result was that poorly paid women working only with other women saw no improvement in their wages. Where it may have been possible, wily employers were able to devise ways of getting round the legislation by intensifying job segregation between the sexes.

In January 1984 amendments to the Act allowing claims for 'equal pay for work of equal value' came into effect, and since then a number of cases have been brought under the new legislation.

Wages Councils

Wages tend to be lower in industries where trade union organisation is weak. Low paid workers therefore have little protection, and the Government's recent proposals for the reform of the Wages Councils threaten to undermine even that. The Wages Councils developed from the Trade Boards set up by Churchill in 1909. Their task is to lay down the legal minimum wage in low-paid industries, mainly retailing, catering, clothing and hairdressing. Twenty-six Wages Councils exist to protect 2·7 million employees (11 per cent of the workforce) in approximately 300,000 workplaces.

In July 1985 the Employment Secretary, Tom King, proposed two main changes to the Wages Councils system which are planned to take effect from June 1986. The first is the removal of young people under 21 from Wages Councils protection. This has possible repercussions for 500,000 young people. The second is the stipulation that Wages Councils can set only a minimum rate of pay and a single overtime rate. Pay differentials could therefore disappear and protection for paid holidays, weekend and shift pay be removed.[10]

The Government's justification for these changes is that the Wages Councils price people, especially young people, out of jobs. It believes that the employment prospects of young people are damaged by the level of their pay relative to adults. Young people's pay is already low in comparison with adults. Since 1979 the pay increases received by young men are 23 per cent lower than the average increase of adult men. Young women's pay increases are 30 per cent behind the equivalent increase for adults generally.[11]

That the present system of Wages Councils has its faults is not really the question. But it is more protection that the workers in low-paid industries need, not less. The level of pay in the Wages Councils sector as a proportion of the national average pay has fallen from 73 per cent in 1974 to 65 per cent in 1984.[12] Now it is certain to fall further.

Since women are heavily concentrated in the Wages Councils sector, they will also be disproportionately affected by the changes, and, with them, their families. The Government's assumption in attacking the wage levels of young people and women is that few young people have family responsibilities and that most women's earnings supplement a man's wage. Therefore, women's low wages do not increase family poverty. This is an illusion. Married women's earnings are often essential to the family budget. The General Household Survey (1978) showed that without the earnings of employed mothers, the proportion of families with an employed father who have a standard of living below the poverty line would rise from 17 per cent to 39 per cent. Increasingly, women are the main or sole wage-earners in their families. This is the case for women with unemployed husbands (over half a million) and for single mothers (about 900,000).

The failure to equalise women's and men's earnings leaves female headed households considerably poorer. The 1974 Finer Report[13] identified low pay of women as the principle cause of poverty in one parent families. In their book, *Despite the Welfare State*, Brown and Madge found

> conclusive evidence that women tend to be worse off than men on virtually all indices of economic status. Households headed by women are, for example, four and a half times as likely as those headed by men to be in poverty . . . The poverty of lone mothers is particularly striking[14]

All in all the number of families living in poverty would quadruple without women's earnings. How is it then possible to deny the link between women's low pay and family poverty?

Women and New Technology

The arrival of new technology holds both disturbing implications and exciting possibilities. On the one hand it can reduce the amount of human labour required, and so, for a time at least, increase unemployment; on the other it can provide the opportunity to do away with much monotonous and dehumanising labour, freeing people to give attention to the more complex and rewarding parts of their work. And yet many of the jobs which are created by the introduction of new technology are themselves dull, boring, and repetitive.

The effects of the introduction of new technology, both on unemployment, and on the nature of work, are not yet fully realised; the recession has discouraged investment in new technology, and so its introduction has not been as speedy as some people originally envisaged. Introducing new technology in one area can rapidly open up further areas to the possibilities of automation or computerisation, and the technology itself is developing as rapidly as the possible applications. The effects will not be at all uniform. The manufacturing and service industries will feel the impact differently. However, in both sectors, women's jobs are drastically effected.

Two million women are employed in the manufacturing industry, and over half of these work as operators and assemblers, the jobs most immediately affected by new technology. In the telegraph and telephone equipment manufacturing industry, the number of assemblers (mostly women) has already been cut by half. New technology can create de-skilled, low-paid jobs, and women who are displaced from semi-skilled assembly work may be forced into them.

In the service industry sector the introduction of word processors and information technology has greatly reduced the demand for unskilled clerical labour. One-third of all employed women work in offices, 90 per cent of them in routine clerical jobs; these women will have little or no access to new jobs if they are displaced. The impact of new technology on office jobs is often at first to lengthen the distinction between those who create, analyse, co-ordinate and interpret the information, and those who merely process it. There are some signs that in subsequent stages this distinction can increasingly break down. If women are not to find themselves once again segregated into the work at the bottom of the scale, then it is essential that they have access to training, to equip them for the new jobs, but also that the job design for the new way of working does not recreate the old distinctions between skilled, semi-skilled, and unskilled.

Homeworking

Probably the most vulnerable and invisible of all employees are the homeworkers, people using their home as a base from which to carry out work—usually piece work—for their employers. Examples of typical jobs done by homeworkers are machining, assembling and painting small toys, sewing buttons onto cards, and addressing envelopes. Most homeworkers are women, and the worst aspects of women's employment are highlighted by the situation of homeworkers—low pay, lack of employment rights, no training prospects, isolation and non-unionisation.

In addition, some homeworking has a dangerous element to it, because it may involve the use of machinery or toxic materials without adequate safeguards.

However, homeworking need not be exploitative. There are, for instance, the new technology homeworkers of which there are a growing number, working on time rates with full employment rights. Most new technology homeworkers are in high status jobs, working as programmers, analysts, project managers and consultants. Only 10 per cent are in clerical occupations (for example, word processor operators), but this percentage is certain to rise with the arrival of cable networks. This kind of homeworking can be an attractive option for employers and employees, given safe and fair conditions. Employers benefit from more productive workers. Employees have control over when they do their work, and may be able to care for children or relatives at home at the same time. The growth of new technology homeworking could be a great boon for disabled people who would find travelling to and from their jobs difficult.

F International Ltd is one example of a successful company which employs homeworkers. It specialises in computer software. Ninety-three per cent of its largely female staff are homeworkers. Their work ranges from consultancy to programming and administrative support. A flexible working pattern means that the employees can arrange their employment to suit their domestic situations.[15]

Traditional homeworkers are the least documented sector of the workforce. Many are excluded from official employment statistics. Fluctuation in the number of homeworkers and their frequent reluctance to declare themselves (because they may be working illegally) makes an accurate estimate of the extent of homeworking extremely difficult to arrive at. Government estimates tend to be modest, implying that it does not exist in a significant way. Other estimates put the figure at half a million or more, and suggest that this is increasing rapidly. Women from ethnic minority groups are particularly likely to seek homeworking. Homeworking may be the only part of the labour market open to them because of language difficulties and cultural restrictions on their public activities.

These homeworkers provide a large, cheap and flexible workforce at the bottom of the economic structure. Employers are often able to save on overheads of site, electricity, equipment, and contributions to national insurance, pension schemes and sick and holiday pay. Overspill from factories offloaded onto homeworkers enables employers to avoid the cost of taking on and laying off permanent staff.

In a sample carried out by the Low Pay Unit,[16] one-third of traditional home-workers interviewed earned 50p an hour or less. Only a quarter earned over £1 an hour. Wages have actually fallen during the last few years, owing to an increase in people willing to take on such work. In an interview recorded in Paul Harrison's book, *Inside the Inner City*, a homeworker from Hackney explains:

I'm having to work twice as hard to earn the money. The governors used to go down on their knees to get you to take work . . . but they're not begging no more. It's take it or leave it. If you argue about the price they say we can always find others to do it. Three years ago we used to get 35·40p a blouse now (1982) you only get 15·20p. Now I work 10 or 12 hours a day—all day really from 3 in the morning to 10 at night. I have to work that long to average £70 a week.[17]

Women and Trade Unions

'A woman's place is in her union' is the newly coined phrase on leaflets, posters and union notice boards. More than a third of trade union membership is female, and women trade unionists are expected to outnumber the men by the end of the decade. But there is little evidence to support this on our television screens or in the union hierarchies. Women's representation on union executives and among full-time officials is poor. A not untypical example is the Union of Shop Distributive and Allied Workers (USDAW). 61 per cent of its members are women, but only one of its eighteen executive members and 5 of its 35 delegates to the Trades Union Congress are women.[18]

It is however encouraging to note the amount of concern within sections of the trade union movement about the under-representation of women and their interests, and about their disadvantaged status as employees. Attempts are being made to appreciate why women resist involvement in unions. Just as women's 'under-achievement' in employment has been viewed as a problem about women rather than about deficiencies in the organisation of their employment, so women's lack of involvement in union activities has often been taken as an indication of their lack of interest in workplace politics and their jobs.

Obstacles to Participation

A closer look at things reveals that there are several factors hindering women's participation. While some are complex, such as those relating to occupational segregation, others, like the time of branch meetings, have straightforward explanations:

(a)   One reason for low unionisation among women workers is that a large proportion of them are employed in workplaces where organisation is far from easy—in small factories and offices, shops or other people's homes, or in industries where labour turnover is high. USDAW,[19] for example, has to recruit one-third of its membership annually simply to maintain its membership level. Often isolated, maybe unaware that their problems are widely experienced, it is difficult for women to congregate or to have a vision of their potential collective strength.

(b)   The concentration of women in low status employment is also relevant. Research shows that a positive correlation exists between higher status work and a high level of union activity.

(c)   Union meetings held out of work hours are difficult for women to attend, particularly if they are part-timers. Lunch-time meetings are also unpopular as many women rely on that time to do shopping. Meetings held during work hours would enable more employees to attend. Where this is not possible due to shift-workers, for example, and meetings are held after work or in the evenings, a crèche is essential.

(d)   The demands of home life was the second most frequent explanation given by men for not being active in their union. How much more will this be the case for women. For them a commitment to union activity makes three jobs instead of two. The trade unions are beginning to recognise domestic work as a trade union issue. Priority needs to be given to devising policies which enable women and men to share responsibility for their homes and children.

(e)   Women do not always see the relevance of trade unions. They will become more involved if unions are seen to reflect their priorities, for example, more flexible working hours and childcare facilities.

Overcoming the Obstacles

Some unions have created special structures to encourage women to participate and voice their interests. These include reserved seats on executive committees and on district and regional committees; the setting up of women-only training courses; the appointment of equal opportunities officers; and the devising of Positive Action Programmes.

Such programmes are not unique to trade unions but have been particularly taken up by them.

The concept of Positive Action recognises the complexity of the factors preventing women from obtaining full rights and opportunities and of the different levels at which discrimination operates. It is a practice which can benefit employers as well as employees. Positive Action Programmes can include designing an Equal Opportunity Policy, broadening the scope of recruitment, providing better training opportunities and allowing for a career break for parents. Because it is a concept which is often misunderstood, it is important to say what Positive Action is not about. It is not about favouring women at men's expense or distributing jobs to women irrespective of merit. Positive Action seeks to make equal opportunities—as enacted by legislation—a real possibility. It is about whatever is necessary to enable women genuinely to compete equally with men and to make full use of opportunities which are nominally there for everybody.

Women's Unemployment

Unemployment for women is not perceived to be the personal and social crisis that it is for men. The visibility of young men on the streets and in centres for the unemployed, the association of masculinity with paid work, the traditional view of the 'breadwinner' role, in a society which generally gives primacy to the male experience, all obscure the reality and hardship of female unemployment.

The impact of the recession in the 1970s was felt most severely in the manufacturing industries and therefore women, who are concentrated in the service sector, were cushioned from the worst effects of the initial decline. Half a million women lost jobs in manufacturing industries between 1961 and 1974, but over this same period two million found them in the expanding service sector. However, as the effects of the recession began to impact upon the service industries and public sector cuts were imposed, women's jobs were axed. The school meals service, for example, employed about 300,000 women on a part-time basis. In 1980 alone, 45,000 of these jobs were lost.

Ethnic Groups

There can be no doubt that black people are particularly vulnerable in times of recession and unemployment. The black population is concentrated in the regions most severely affected, and the industries on which they have relied for employment have suffered dramatic decline. An example is the textile industry which provided jobs for large numbers of Asian women. The occupational inequality between black and white people is another reason why black people are more susceptible to unemployment. But these factors do not account for the much higher unemployment rates among black people. Racial prejudice and institutional racism play their part.

The economic activities of women vary according to their ethnic and cultural background. More West Indian women (74 per cent) are in or seeking employment than white or Asian women (46 per cent and 39 per cent). A wide variety of practice is found among Asian groups, with Muslim women much less likely to be economically active than other Asian women (18 per cent as compared with 57 per cent). Activity rates among Asians are strongly related to their ability to speak English. A greater proportion of West Indian and Asian women in employment are in full time jobs than is the case for white women. 44 per cent of white women are 'part-timers'. The figures for West Indian and Asian women are 29 per cent and 16 per cent respectively.[20]

Unemployment for white women currently stands at 10 per cent. For West Indian women it is 16 per cent and for Asian women 20 per cent. In all three groups there are thousands more women who are not registered as unemployed, but who are looking for jobs. The number of black women who count as long-term unemployed is double that of white women.

Registration

In 1971 women made up 17 per cent of the registered unemployed in the UK. Today they account for 30 per cent of the registered unemployed. There were 984,000 unemployed women claimants, excluding school leavers, in July 1985, in comparison with 346,000 in 1979.[21]

The official statistics relating to female unemployment in this country do not reflect the full extent of the problem. In 1981 the General Household Survey found that 41 per cent of unemployed married women, and 16 per cent of unemployed single women were not officially registered as unemployed.[22] From October 1982 changes in the method of collecting statistics further obscured the level of unemployment among women. Previously it sufficed to register at a Job Centre to be counted as unemployed, but the changes meant that only those in receipt of unemployment benefit were registered as unemployed. Many married women, desperately looking for a job, experiencing all the problems of unemployment but not eligible for benefit, were wiped out of the picture and became invisible. Not even a statistic. *Labour Research* in December 1982 estimated that the number of unemployed women in the UK was double the government figure.

Unemployment in the European community is significantly higher amongst women than for men. The UK statistics would appear to provide an exception to the rule. But because the UK has more stringent registration procedures than the other member states, the reality is not likely to be any different.

Motherhood as a Way Out?

All a woman really wants is a husband, home and children! So runs the myth, but sadly, in the absence of meaningful alternatives there is evidence to suggest that many women are prematurely opting for marriage and motherhood. To say this is in no way to imply that marriage and motherhood are not worthy occupations, but they must be chosen freely and not as a last desperate resort.

> Beatrix Campbell found on her travels that 'one of the first things you notice in Northern cities hit by unemployment is babies, lots of babies with very young parents...it is an alternative to aimless adolescence on the dole'. A Sunderland woman explained to her, 'It's part of becoming a member of the community instead of just a reckless teenager. You don't need to get a job when you're a Mam. When you're a Mam somebody needs you'.[23]

The effect of government policy and much public opinion is to make married women feel that they have no legitimate right to work. Government ministers seem to believe that a married woman's place is out of the labour market and in the home. This belief is reflected in the policy of the Manpower Services Commission. Women who cannot claim benefit are ineligible for government job creation schemes because applicants must be taken from the unemployment register. In October 1984 this proviso was extended to the Community Programme which was providing many married women with part-time employment.[24] The message is plain: men's jobs are the priority.

'Weed out the working wives' advised the *Daily Mail* in 1977, and thereby reduce male unemployment. A frequently voiced belief is that women take men's jobs. This is another myth. Is a redundant miner going to take on part-time, low paid domestic work? The sexual division of labour is so rigid that, by and large, the patterns of female and male unemployment have followed the fortunes of 'female' and 'male' industries. Where an industry employs both women and men, women are more vulnerable to redundancy, because they tend to be less well-trained and so more easily replaced. Besides, it should not be necessary to defend women against the accusation that they take men's jobs. Preference should not be given to men's needs over against those of women. A person's right to employment should not depend on their sex.

It has been clearly demonstrated that the cards are heavily stacked against women in the world of employment. Discrimination means elevating the concerns of one group over another; it results in inequality of pay, opportunity and status. Christians are right in feeling uneasy about such a situation. A Christian commitment to justice and equality means challenging a society which resists its realisation. Such a commitment will express itself in the search for a society in which equal consideration is given to the various needs of all groups and people.

Chapter Three

WOMEN AND WORK—UNSEEN, UNPAID

The tensions between the demands made by home and workplace are disproportionately born by women; their primary sphere is seen to be in the home, even when they are in full-time employment. To discuss women's employment in isolation will give us only half the picture. If we are to understand the 'under achievement' of women in the world of paid work, and the obstacles facing them, we must understand more about their other area of activity, which is less open to public scrutiny—the home. Women generally organise their paid work in order to inconvenience their families as little as possible and this greatly affects their employment opportunities. For many, this means part-time work, with its attendant disadvantages. Others try to find jobs close at hand, in order to avoid spending precious time travelling.

Women still carry out most of the work that is necessary for the maintenance of home and raising of children. Many are also involved in caring for elderly or disabled relatives. It is to these two areas of housework and 'caring' which we now turn.

Housework

Although more women have paid jobs than ever before, there has not been a corresponding increase in men's contribution to housework. The demands made of women who labour under a dual burden of paid and unpaid work are considerable. When they leave their workplace they are merely switching from one shift to another.

Housework is the major occupation of women. Its isolated, repetitive and unending nature can make it an unrewarding occupation, concerned with maintenance not creation. It is easily trivialised by those who do not do any and who seem to regard being a housewife as a leisure activity. Because it is carried out in isolation when other family members are absent, housework is invisible and therefore the time and energy expended on it goes unacknowledged. A sample study by Ann Oakley in 1971[1] revealed that housewives did an average of 77 hours work a week. Labour saving devices have not reduced the amount of time spent on housework. Women interviewed by Ann Oakley for her booklet evidently experienced housework as hard work and objected to the low status attached to their occupation which is classed as non-work.

> I'm not married to a house. I hate the word 'housewife'. They say 'What are you?' and I say 'I've got a baby . . . I'm a mother and a wife', and they say 'Oh, just a housewife'. Just a housewife! The hardest job in the world. You're never just a housewife. Into that category comes everything.[2]

Women who are 'just housewives' are defined by the General Registrar's Office as 'Others Economically Inactive'. They are regarded as being economically dependent upon their partners. In being responsible for her family's well-being, however, the housewife is producing something that is essential to our economy—its 'workers'. How many men in employment would be able to work the number of hours they do if they had to feed, clothe and generally care for themselves and their children?

'Behind every great man there stands a great woman' goes the old cliché, and we hear the overworked career woman quip that what she needs is a wife—that is, someone to do her shopping, cooking and ironing. How many men owe their public success to their wives' unpaid contributions to their work—not only the servicing, but in many cases the entertaining and secretarial duties?[3] There is little public acknowledgement of the backup workers' essential contribution to social and economic production. It takes place behind closed doors and not in the public eye. Janet Finch argues that:

> one of the effects of treating work and home as separate spheres and assuming that productive work takes place only in the former is to obscure the extent to which household activities and especially the performance of domestic labour are economic activities.[4]

Costs

The Legal and General Insurance Company estimated recently that the commercial value of the work done by a woman in the home as laundress, cook, childminder, and nurse, is, on average, £227·23 a week.[5] Some people argue that women should be paid for their housework. The danger in the idea of 'wages for housework' is that present 'feminine/masculine' roles could become further entrenched, and that men might feel justified in withdrawing their help in the home altogether. However, the idea pinpoints two important things. First it recognises that housework is WORK. Until it is regarded as work, an occupation as demanding and valid as any other, housewives will continue to have none of the rights or status accruing to other workers. The most fundamental of these rights is time off. If you do not work you do not need time off from your work. Numerous women are never 'off duty'. Secondly, the idea of wages for housework recognises that housework is undervalued. Our society pays for what it values. Therefore, to pay for a service is the way to ensure that it is valued. It would also give more choice to women (and men) who might prefer to stay and work at home rather than seek outside employment.

Caring

Discussion about the caring responsibilities of women has tended to revolve solely around their role as mothers. Within the last few years, increasing light has been shed upon their role as carers for the disabled, ill and elderly. The portrayal of our society as uncaring, neglectful and in need of a dose of good old Victorian values is partial and distorted. Instances of abuse are well publicised. What we do not hear about or see are the private struggles of individual carers who have little recourse to external support systems, but who meet, day in day out, the time-consuming physical and emotional demands of a dependent.

A small door-to-door study in Newcastle by the Association of Carers (1983)[6] produced the staggering statistic that 1 in 4 women over 25 were carers, and that there were more people caring for dependent relatives than there were people caring for children under 16. An Equal Opportunities Commission Survey (1982)[7] revealed that three-quarters of carers are women, mostly married and in their 40s and 50s. Caring is rarely a short-term commitment. 49 per cent of carers interviewed by the Commission had been caring from 1–4 years at the time of interview. 20 per cent had spent 5–9 years and 12 per cent 10–14 years in their caring roles.

The increase in the number of elderly people as a proportion of the population means that more caring is going to be required of fewer potential carers.[8] There are 10 times as many over-85s as there were 80 years ago, but there are now fewer single women with no children or no employment outside the home—those who traditionally have been expected to do the caring. These changes will result in a larger burden of unpaid work for women.

The Government's public expenditure cuts exacerbate the problem. The phrase 'care in/by the community' is little more than a euphemism for unpaid work by women, since communities now have fewer resources with which to care. The care of children and of the elderly is a family responsibility, a private concern, and therefore something to be left well alone by the State. By defining them as private issues, the State is spared the task of providing widespread support services. By being 'private issues' they also automatically become 'women's issues'.

The financial costs of caring are heavy. Women are more likely than men to give up a job to care for a relative. That means loss of income, a reduced pension and additional expenses required to meet their relatives' special needs. Then there are the personal costs to the carer: stress, isolation and restriction of activity, the forgoing of opportunities for fulfilment through employment. Many women have just finished raising their children when an elderly relative falls ill and their hopes of concentrating on their employment are dashed. Their lives are lives of continual caring—for children, then for elderly parents and then for their spouse or companion.

Discrimination and Stereotyping

The Invalid Care Allowance (ICA)[9] is the one benefit specifically designed to assist carers, but it is denied to the majority of them—married women. Men and single women who give up jobs to care for relatives are entitled to the allowance. Married women are not, on the grounds that married women are economically dependent on their husbands. The policy for the distribution of this allowance is directly discriminating against married women.

Our European partners are challenging Britain over this injustice. A Social Security Appeals Tribunal recently ruled that the distribution of the Invalid Care Allowance is in breach of the European Economic Community's directive on equal treatment in social security payments.

The policy demonstrates how the State considers the choice between paid work and unpaid caring to be a quite different issue for men than for married women. Loss of employment is thought to be more costly for men, because 'work' is a normal male activity and a right. For women 'work' is granted as a favour and thought to be of less personal importance than it is for a man. The case of the ICA distribution exemplifies how social policies are founded upon certain assumptions about 'normal' relationships and masculine and feminine roles. In a 'normal' family a male breadwinner supports a non-earning wife and children. Yet such normal families account for only 5 per cent of all households.

Psychological arguments that women are more suited to domestic and caring work than men must be resisted. Women's over-work as homemakers and carers is not born of a natural, effortless predisposition, but of necessity. Women are being asked to bear the brunt of the crisis we are in. Their work overload is not inevitable; it is a product of the way society organises itself. It could be changed if we chose.

In the world of paid work, our society has different expectations of women and men and sets different standards for them. This division and inequality is reproduced in the domestic world, the invisible sphere of women. A woman's paid work, whatever else its deficiencies, receives at least a modicum of public recognition in the form of a wage. Her unpaid labour receives none.

The proper care of children, the disabled and elderly is among the most important work carried out by society. Most of it is done by women. Yet they receive scant public assistance. That financial help and practical backup is so restricted and that so little status is attached to the work reflects a gross distortion of society's values.

Women's Employment and Social Policy

A society committed to promoting equality of opportunity between the sexes needs to consider what changes are required, in terms of social policy, to achieve this. It should be questioning social policies which assume that women and men have different priorities, and which make different demands of them—as in the case of the distribution of Invalid Care Allowance. It should be supporting adjustments in employment practices which enable people to combine their employment with domestic responsibilities. There is little evidence to indicate that these concerns are close to the heart of the present Government.

The most important service required by employed parents is the public provision of childcare. This is overwhelmingly inadequate in the UK. Inadequate childcare provision restricts the employment of at least 35 per cent of mothers with dependent children.[9]

A high percentage of women interviewed by the Department of Employment used family-based childcare. The grandmother was the most common carer of children whose mother worked full-time. 'The paid labour of women is still heavily dependent on the unpaid labour of other women'.[10]

Two per cent of all employed women in the Department of Employment survey had access to a day nursery or crèche run by the local authority and social services. Four per cent had children under 5 in a state nursery school or class. 'The use of formal institutional care such as crèches, day nurseries or nursery classes was relatively rare, reflecting their limited availability.'[11]

Chapter Four

INDUSTRIALISATION AND THE CHANGING ROLE OF WOMEN

Why is there a marked division of labour between men and women in our society?

Anthropological studies show that, while maleness and femaleness are biological facts, masculinity and femininity are largely cultural creations, reflecting the attitudes, values and organisation of specific societies. It is contended below that, historically, the sexual division of labour has intensified as a society has become more industrialised. Since this division of labour is a significant cause of sexual inequality some of the origins of the present predicament of women can be looked for in the process of industrialisation.

To treat this explanation as a key to open all doors would be simplistic. The sexual division of labour is not the only cause or explanation of sexism, but it is easier to investigate than its other suggested roots. There is some value, therefore, in looking at the hypothesis that the division of labour is more rigid in industrialised societies. Not least it challenges the common naivety which regards women's 'progress' as a straightforward move from the closet of the home into the modern world of work.

In pre-industrial societies fewer boundaries mapped out the parameters between public, professional and business life, and the domestic and private. The values and aptitudes appropriate to the one were also appropriate to the other. Although some tasks may have been monopolised by one sex—and Margaret Mead argues[1] that those done by men automatically had higher status—yet, women's work was essential for the efficient running of the home economy.

The home was the workplace, the centre of production, and all members of the family would be engaged in its labour. Women were fully involved in agriculture and textiles, the two major occupations in pre-industrial society. They ploughed, harvested, thatched, sheared sheep and wove. All these tasks were necessary to domestic life.

With industrialisation and the move to the towns came the gradual geographical separation of home and workplace. Production was moved from the home to the factory. Whereas previously shopkeepers' homes were also their shops, they now chose to have separate premises. Separate accounts for home and business began to be kept. Goods for private consumption and public exchange no longer came from the same source. Household labour began to lose its obvious connection with the production of goods and, therefore, it lost some of its recognition. The home became primarily a consumer and child raising unit. This change in women's activities resulted in a change in status. For the first time, women became economically dependent upon men, and were perceived as marginal to production.

The harsh realities of industrial urban life prompted the Victorian middle-class idealisation of the home as a haven from the ills of a wicked world—a private sphere acting as a buffer against sordid city life. Women were seen to embody homely virtues—comforting and serene. To keep women thus uncontaminated, they had to be protected from the public world. This ideal was unrealistic for most working-class people. For the middle-class male, a non-working wife indicated professional success. He did not need his wife to work, but could 'keep her'.

The revolution in work patterns was preceded and accompanied by corresponding shifts in family structures. The extended family of grand-parents, aunts, uncles and cousins gradually broke up and was replaced by smaller family units. The 'nuclear family', which society today takes so much for granted, arose as a result of these and other changes (such as more effective methods of contraception).

Two Distinct Spheres

All this led to the defining of two distinct spheres—public and private, workplace and home, wage and unwaged—his and hers. Two different sets of behaviour are required for operation in either of these spheres, because the spheres are based on two different kinds of social relationship. From the woman in the home, what is required is gentleness, placidity and altruism. From men fighting in the 'real world', competitiveness, aggressiveness and hardness are the necessary qualities which ensure survival and success.

The Church did not escape this split. It is apparent in the way in which religion became privatised and sentimentalised in the nineteenth century. The Church saw its task as promoting the qualities of women and the home. Jesus—gentle, meek and mild—becomes 'womanly', an example of self-effacement. Few traces of anger, confrontation and challenge are found in Victorian representations of him. The Church's twentieth century self-understanding as a family means that its main involvement and interest has been with private morals and individual concerns.

We can see some of the consequences of the split in our society today, in our perceptions about work and ourselves as people. One of these is the distinction already noted earlier in the last chapter between paid, productive work and unpaid, domestic work, the latter often not recognised as work at all. The former is invested with a value and visibility which the latter does not have, and the connections between them are not made.

Some of women's paid servicing work occupies a fuzzy area between the two spheres (for instance, cleaning offices). On the one hand, it is paid and so belongs to the public arena. On the other hand it is an extension of work done in the home, but done outside normal employment hours, and done by women. In this respect it is private. It is not part of the 'main action'.[2]

It is worth noting that a great deal of women's activity is defined as being outside the 'main action'; caring for children before they go to school and enter the 'action', or caring for the elderly and sick, those who have retired from the 'action'. Historically it seems that once an activity is defined as part of the 'main action' and is professionalised, trained and waged it is automatically no longer the concern of women. An example of this is medicine, for centuries in the sphere of women, but by the eighteenth or nineteenth-century completely taken over by men.

Another consequence of this compartmentalisation is the way in which women and men may be restricted by being expected to identify too closely with either the private or public sphere. Too close an identification with a particular role or sphere makes people particularly vulnerable if that role is questioned or removed. People are encouraged to identify with the private or public sphere according to their sex. Women are identified with the home, although they are seen to make forays out into the public world of employment. Men are identified with life outside the home, although they are acknowledged to retreat into it. They are in danger of disintegration if their source of identity is taken away. A man who has derived his meaning and self-respect from his employment will be especially hard hit by redundancy. A woman who has built her identity upon her role as wife and mother may feel she has lost her essence when her children leave home or if her marriage breaks up.

Finally, the public/private split causes and perpetuates women's reliance upon men in both spheres. It withholds from them self-determination and independence. The value and visibility of the public over the private means that women frequently have to resort to male patronage in order to gain a stake in the world of public employment, and the overall stronger economic

position of men gives them control over the private sphere too. In both spheres there is an inequality of power, society's affirmation of male superiority.

This argument may need refining, but it does help us understand why women and men are seen to have such divergent priorities and interests. It accounts in part for the way in which our thinking about life has become compartmentalised.

We are living during a period which in retrospect may appear as momentous to our descendants as the Industrial Revolution does to us. A return to full employment given present trends seems to be little more than a pipe dream for the foreseeable future, and new styles of life and work need to be developed. Men's unemployment reintroduces them into the home. The introduction of cable networks means that more people will be carrying out their work from home. We see on our television screens how what we do in the West has world-wide repercussions. We are able to make the connections. Are we reintegrating the public and private spheres? Can this reintegration be seen as a positive development which will promote human wholeness?

Part Two

Chapter Five

INTRODUCTION

The task of reflecting upon and learning about God and human experience can never be said to be complete. Theology has to be open-ended, inviting the possibility of new insights arising from fresh experiences. If theology is to be relevant to the present, it needs to be more than a revamped theology from yesterday. Making sense of our present needs is what is at stake.

It must also respond to the needs of women, to have their experience recognised and taken seriously. Women's lives are worthwhile material for theology. Their experience is significantly different from men's. Out of it they are raising questions about and offering new perspectives on work, values, peace, ways of organising change, and ways of relating to one another. Theology needs to draw on women's distinctive contribution, but it is challenging. There is nothing very easy or comfortable in facing up to it. Nothing is more unsettling than having question marks placed over embedded patterns of behaviour and deeply cherished beliefs.

The Church—along with everyone else—has a choice to make concerning these questions. It can ignore them; or it can accept their uncomfortable presence and learn to live with them in the most creative way possible. If the Church takes this option—and we hope it will—there are a number of areas which would repay attention. Part Two will focus on three of these areas. Whilst highlighting these central themes, we recognise that others, which might have been included, have had to be left out. However, these three themes arise most urgently from Part One of the report. We believe they should be priorities for Christians.

The first, not suprisingly, is that of sexual justice which, as Part One has demonstrated, is still a long way off. It is important to discuss how we understand sexual justice in order to avoid misunderstanding and to spell out its implications for women and men—not only in terms of the redistribution of resources, but in terms of opportunities for self-expression and fulfilment.

The second area we look at is work. Two useful and familiar concepts theologians have used in discussions about work are 'servanthood' and 'stewardship'. We must reflect on these in the light of women's experience of work and to free from them negative connotations and limited understandings.

Finally, but most urgently, the Church has to look at itself. How does it treat its own women? How will it have to adjust its understanding of people, itself, of God and God's Kingdom?

Before examining these three areas it is necessary to describe briefly the fundamental convictions underlying these arguments and the implications that they have for theological method.

Underlying Convictions

The sources to be drawn upon for the development of theology are numerous, since anything that contributes to a deeper understanding of the human condition has something to offer to theology. All theologians, therefore, make choices about the sources they use, the disciplines from which they draw, and the experiences to which they give weight. They have to develop criteria by which these choices are made and they must be prepared to state and justify these criteria.

As a central part of the Christian tradition, the Scriptures are a key source for the development of theology. Yet with this source too, it is necessary to recognise the selective process which occurs in the formulation of theology and the limitations of such selectivity. Many urgent contemporary issues did not present themselves to the Jews or early Christian Church and the assumption that we can easily formulate a 'biblical' view on them is mistaken. The different historical and cultural contexts in which the Bible was put together should prevent us from drawing simple analogies between events described in it and those of today. In addition, there is by no means agreement on many issues in the Bible. That is why it is possible to use or misuse the Bible to justify so many opposing standpoints—from inciting rebellion to upholding the status quo and all options inbetween.

Yet despite all the problems, the Scriptures remain the major Christian source for theology.

Furthermore, it can be argued that the Bible yields a basic orientation which can offer a self-correcting set of principles to guide us in our use of it and in the determining of Christian action. For instance, a prominent theme, running especially through the teaching of the prophets and of Jesus, is God's concern for disadvantaged and exploited people and intention to bring about a new, just order. Adopting this as a theological criterion means that passages which appear to uphold unjust status and privilege are not seen as authoritative.

The feminist perspective adds another dimension to the discussion about theological method. Feminist theologians are likely to find the Bible problematic. Written by men in a culture created and ruled by men it has been used over the centuries to subordinate women. Since feminist theologians adopt a variety of methods in their interpretation of the Bible, it is necessary to outline the method we have adopted here.

Essentially we are using the self-correcting principle mentioned above, bearing in mind that women make up the majority of disadvantaged and exploited human beings. The principle starts with the conviction that women are fully human and require to be recognised and treated as such. Whatever diminishes women and makes them of less account than men is to be resisted as contrary to God's will. Whatever promotes women's full humanity focuses God's image in them more clearly.

Chapter Six

JUSTICE

A commitment to social justice is not an optional extra for Christians. It cannot be disregarded by anyone who claims to take their discipleship seriously and seeks, in obedience to Jesus' words, to 'love your neighbour as yourself'. The parable of the Good Samaritan shows that no one is beyond such love and neighbourly concern; it affirms God's involvement with all people. As far as God is concerned, our identity as human beings is more fundamental than our religious, racial or sexual identity. This is the truth which finds expression at various points in the biblical and Christian tradition. It triumphs over the sectarian inclinations of the Pharisees and the Jewish Christians to reach its zenith in St Paul's famous words 'in Christ there is neither Jew nor Greek, there is neither slave nor free, there is neither male nor female' (Galatians 3.28).

This may be our goal. In Christ, differences are not to be eroded nor treated as insignificant; it is impossible to be a person without a sexual, racial or religious identity. But such differences should not be treated as the basis for privilege. All too often they are used to justify unfair distribution of resources, status and power, and to create personal and group relationships based upon dominance and subordination.

Such relationships have been the subject of much anthropological and psychological investigation. Dominant groups describe subordinate groups as possessing those characteristics which are not part of their own self image—being emotional, passive, indecisive, and weak. Dominant groups monopolise the functions to which most value is attached and prescribe other servicing roles to their inferiors. These roles are then justified by talk of 'natural differences'. Any questioning of, or protest about, these arrangements is seen as threatening anarchy. Objects are ignored, ridiculed or crushed according to the perceived extent of the threat. These observations about the behaviour of dominant groups are useful in exploring sexism. Many of the arguments which are used to justify sexist practices can be seriously questioned when it is seen that the same arguments are used by other dominant groups to maintain their position.

The Experience of Women

The Women's Movement has arisen because of the injustices women feel they have experienced at the hands of a dominant group. Their identity is viewed as inferior to men's, and they are often relegated to the status of second-class human beings. This is reflected in social arrangements which deny them self-determination and influence, and exclude them from full participation in society by confining them to narrow spheres of activity. It is maintained that these arrangements are appropriate, because physiological and psychological differences between the sexes equip them for the respective role laid upon them. Only 'unnatural' people can object to such arrangements—'unfeminine' women and 'unmasculine' men.

Justice becomes an issue because opportunities and resources are so unequally distributed. Men seem to have priority over women, in terms of access to resources, employment, status and opportunity. It is not that women want everybody to be treated exactly alike or to have exactly the same things—that is to trivialise the issue. To demand justice is to demand that everyone's wellbeing should receive equal consideration, and that in the distribution of resources and the planning of social structures no group or individual should be given undue precedence over another. This would mean several things for women.

Women's Rights

First, women's rights are as important as the rights of all other groups, and are not to be sacrificed in hard times. Women, in Britain and across the world, are often particularly vulnerable in hard times. Smaller earnings over a lifetime cause poverty in old age; one-parent families are mostly headed by women; and mothers in poor families are usually the ones who go without, in order that others can have more. So long as women have less access to resources, they will remain economically dependent upon men, and continue in an unfair and unequal relationship to them in home and employment.

Impressions and Prejudices

Secondly, general impressions and prejudices—which argue that women are unsuited to certain activities because of their sex—cannot be allowed to continue. A woman's suitability for an activity should be tested by her ability, not by the ability of women generally. It may or may not be true at the moment that men are generally more suited to become engineers than are women. But all differences between the sexes are differences on average. On average men may make better engineers than women, but there are certainly individual women who make better engineers than individual men. These women, the engineering industry and all those who benefit from it lose out if their skills are not used.

Co-Creators with God

Thirdly, all people, women and men, are called to be co-creators with God, and thus to participate in the shaping of society and the making of history. The expectation is that women should have to make it in a man's world. They are expected to adopt the man-made structures in society and the Church rather than to recreate them to take into account their needs and preferences. This expectation denies women the fulfilment of their calling, and thwarts God's purposes too.

This call to co-creation reflects the gregarious nature of human beings. People need each other. Relationships must be about giving and receiving if they are not to be exploitative and dehumanising. Imbalance in relationships diminishes, by investing men with the power to control lives other than their own. It diminishes women by keeping them dependent and limiting their self-determination.

The Bible and Sexual Justice

What support is there for this ideal of sexual justice amongst biblical and Christian sources? The creation stories in Genesis contain basic truths on this theme. A consideration of the origins and purposes of God's creation reveals humanity's hopeful destiny. The stories of the creation and the vision of new life in Christ point to the same truth—that women and men are united beyond any differences.

There are two creation stories in Genesis. The one which comes first in our text (Genesis 1–2.4) speaks of men and women being made in God's image. 'Male and female he created them.' (Genesis 1.27). God's image is therefore incomplete without both male and female. Together they are God's representatives on earth. In the second story (Genesis 2.4 following) Adam is created first and then Eve. Adam plays no part in her creation, since he is in a deep sleep at the time. He recognises himself in Eve. She is not 'the other':

this at last is bone of my bone and flesh of my flesh (Genesis 2.23).

Eve is not a secondary addition to the human race, but completes and fulfils it. The word 'helper' (Hebrew—ezer), used to describe Eve's relation to Adam, should not be taken to mean subordination, since elsewhere in the Bible it describes God's relation to Israel.

Then comes the Fall. One of its consequences, for Eve, is that 'he shall rule over you'. (Genesis 3.16.) Male domination is part of the fallen order, not of the original divine intention. It is a product and cause of sin. In an unfallen world there would be not injustice and enmity between women and men. Harmony between them will be one outcome of the restoration of creation to its original state.

The coming of the new Adam, Christ, proclaims the passing away of this old order and the inauguration of a new one. If anyone is in Christ s/he is a new creation, refusing to conform to the world's values and practices. All this should mean that Christians stand out because of their freedom from sexism. It is ironic that instead Christianity is the epitomy of misogyny to many.

The new order is one in which old structures of domination and subjugation are questioned and struggled with. By refusing to validate existing oppressive social and religious hierarchies God stands firmly on the side of the vulnerable, poor and oppressed and against the current pattern of unequal social relationships. Nowhere is God's commitment more clearly in evidence than in the resurrection of Jesus. The resurrection—the start of that new life—must be understood as God's way of vindicating the very lifestyle and behaviour of Jesus which led to his being arrested, tried and crucified as a trouble-maker, rabble-rouser and blasphemer.

This behaviour included an utterly different approach to women than that of his Jewish contemporaries. Mary Evans, in her investigation of what the Bible has to say about women and their role in society, describes Jesus' approach to women, as described in the Gospels, as revolutionary.

> Jesus healed women, he allowed them to touch him and to follow him; he spoke without restraint of women, to women and with women. He related to women primarily as human beings rather than as sexual beings, that is, he was interested in them as persons, seeing their sex as an integral part but by no means the totality of their personality.[1]

> One feature of all four gospels which goes a long way towards authenticating the story (of the resurrection) as a whole is the prominence of women; for this is a feature which the early Church would not be likely to invent.[2]

The prominence of women in the accounts of Jesus' resurrection is highly significant:

> Women are primarily presented in these accounts as witnesses. To the Jews, the evidence given by women was of no account. The events of the crucifixion and resurrection make it quite clear that for Christians this can never be so.[3]

We can understand God's 'bias to the poor' as also a 'bias to women'—not on account of their sex, but because women make up the majority of the vulnerable.

These reflections about the purpose and fulfilment of creation and redemption stem from a fundamental conviction about justice which should influence and underlie Christian thought and practice. Such a conviction is sharply reinforced by the life of Jesus of Nazareth, whose attitude to women contrasted so powerfully with his contemporaries'. The coming reign of God, already present and active in Jesus, includes and endorses women as equal partners in the human vocation to serve and shape the world for God and good. While men do the lion's share of defining and shaping society, the insights and performances of women are lost. In order for them to have an equal place in the world, women must find their own voice with which to break the silence.

Chapter Seven

STEWARDSHIP AND SERVANTHOOD

As we have already noted, women's experience of work is significantly different from men's and therefore requires separate and serious analysis in our theology. Much material has been produced under the broad heading of 'Theology of Work'. But it has not sufficiently addressed women's experience of work. For example, no treatment of women's work can equate work solely with paid employment, thereby ignoring housework which is a principle occupation of nearly all women in our society. It is imperative to redefine work in order to render visible the invisible unpaid work done by women.

Stewardship

We want to express the hopeful conviction that humanity is in a co-operative relationship with God, and also that with God humanity is engaged upon a joint venture, the stewardship of the earth. These two elements appear to be the key to what the writer of Genesis meant in speaking of humanity being made in God's image. A primary purpose of work is that we should mirror God the creator in the creative use of our gifts and in the shaping of the world. The monotonous and dehumanising nature of many jobs points to our failure to live up to this vision.

Servanthood

The idea of stewardship is closely linked with that of servanthood. This idea needs reclaiming in our thinking, because servanthood carries associations of submission, inferiority and powerlessness. Servants are given the work which, although acknowledged to be essential, is regarded as beneath the dignity of their rulers to do; but servanthood can be seen as something which is voluntarily assumed, an indication of the person's commitment to others. It is an acknowledgement of the identification of the servant with the ones s/he serves, a service freely chosen out of strength, not forced or compromised out of weakness. Such service asks for recognition, though it cannot force it. We derive satisfaction and self-respect largely from valuing the work we do and from being valued for it.

Men's experience is illuminated by these considerations, as well as women's. However, particular challenges begin to emerge when applied to the reality of women's work.

Stewardship of Resources

The responsible stewarding of resources in the service of humanity involves making decisions about the importance of the work there is to be done and the effective use of people's abilities in doing it. We fail if we set ourselves a false set of priorities. Much of the paid work done in our society bears little relation to the meeting of human needs. We also fail if we squander people's talents.

A common understanding of Christian teaching and stewardship is that it is chiefly concerned with the individual's attitude to possessions and use of time and money. This should be balanced by emphasising that the scope of our stewardship extends to people too. We need to think of stewardship in terms of the proper care of dependents, the education of our children and the meeting of common human needs. In this sense, it is mainly women who have been stewards. Over the last 200 years many men have had little energy left to share these responsibilities after long shifts of manual work. With the changes in patterns of employment, men have more opportunity to do this stewarding. Some are rediscovering the importance of this work, and taking more part in the upbringing of their children. This is a very positive indication that gender roles are breaking down and that people are finding new ways of relating to one another—and, ironically, mass unemployment has not been irrelevant to this.

Meeting people's needs can be repetitive and dull with little scope for personal development. That is another reason why, in the interests of the correct stewarding of people's gifts, caring needs to be shared, and supplemented by more varied work. For too long, however, women have been told that their talents equip them for motherhood, caring and servicing alone, that they must seek fulfilment through this work and that other goals are deviations from their true vocation. This is in no way to deny the importance of such work. For many women, enormous satisfaction is found in years of caring work as a wife and mother. However, a woman's biological role in reproduction ought not to be rationalised into a lifetime of servicing work which does not cater for her need to develop herself, her abilities and so to make her contribution in other ways to society.

Caring for dependents and other forms of creative work need not be mutually exclusive options. That they are for so many women is an indictment of society:

> it is no part of Feminism to insist that a woman should work at other things even though her children suffer as a consequence, but it is part of Feminism to insist that there is something radically wrong with a system which forces so many women to choose between caring properly for their children and using their abilities fully.[1]

Calling to Servanthood

The Christian calling includes the call to servanthood, but the response to that calling must be a free one. Presumably the Church would wish to argue that it is through this Christian calling that people find and fulfil themselves. Service must entail the personal growth of the servant as well as the welfare of those served.

Women's service must not make them into an enslaved class. Service embraces many activities and not simply those which are at the lower end of the occupational scale. Women must be free to choose their response to the call to service, and that response will be one which caters for their own needs and abilities as well as those of others. For women servanthood has not always been compatable with finding themselves. 'Women have now stated that helping in the growth of others without the equal opportunity and right to growth for themselves is a form of oppression'.[2]

The Church too often associates servanthood with meekness and self-negation and sets these as ideals for women. The distinction between service and subservience has to be made. Subservience is not a Christian virtue.

Women's paid work tends to be low paid and therefore undervalued. Women's unpaid work receives little recognition at all. If the necessary assistance for carers is withheld, it is hardly suprising that this is interpreted as a refusal to recognise the demands that are made on them and the social importance of their work. Lip service is not enough. Valuing a person's work never means overlooking it. If housewives and carers are without status and their work not properly valued, it means that society has the wrong values, because the task of caring for others is one of the most important.

> As long as the people who excel in the most important work are without status, it means that society undervalues their work, and as long as that happens society has the wrong values. Valuing is not the sort of thing which vaguely goes on at the back of people's minds on Sundays, when they allow their minds to

wander to the worthiness of obscure people who do good work. What it means for a society to value what is good is for it to reward what is good, and until virtue is rewarded it means that the right things are not.

Janet Radcliffe Richards[3]

Chapter Eight

WOMEN AND WORK—AND THE CHURCH

The different ways in which men and women understand and experience work reflect the division which our society makes between the public, corporate, political world of work and the private, personal, world of 'home and family'. It is vitally important to challenge this separation. If God's concern is with the whole of life—with work, relationships and politics—then the Church must not submit to the tendency to fragment people into roles and the world into water-tight compartments. Partly as a result of industrialisation and 'secularisation', the public sphere is seen to have severed its links with God and the sacred. The Church has become privatised in as much as its primary function is seen to be the care of individual souls. Arguably it has also become 'feminised' in that it nurtures the values and attitudes with which women are especially associated. When Church leaders comment on political matters, they are stepping over the boundary between 'private' and 'public' and soon get their knuckles rapped.

This boundary must be crossed. For if it is not, the truth is not being told about the realities of people's lives, about the effects which public policies and public attitudes have on individual aspirations and circumstances. The Church must not lose sight of its role of pronouncing judgement on unjust social and political structures, because these structures tell people very clearly what they are and how much or little they are worth. The powerful must not be spared the task of morally scrutinising what they do. And no one should evade the responsibility of challenging unjust structures by thinking they can have no effect on anything that takes place outside their front door.

'The personal is political' is one of the primary insights of the Women's Movement. That is, the 'private' is 'public' and the 'public' is 'private'. What I do personally has wider implications than for me alone, and what happens 'out there' has direct results for me.

Because the Church has traditionally been associated with the private sphere it can have an important part to play in reclaiming and revaluing its activities and its values for everybody, for use in the public world of employment and in politics. It can reclaim the work which women do in the home as part of the 'main action' of society, and it can argue that the so-called feminine attributes are those which are needed in order to create a more just and humane society.

The Role of Women in the Church

Last summer, a group of Church women spent a week together at the Iona Community. What does it feel like, they were asked, to be a woman in the Church? They each drew pictures to sum up their perceptions. For one woman, the Church was a 'top heavy' pyramid. In the bottom part was a woman's mouth crossed out. In the top part was a man's ear, also crossed out. Another drawing showed stick women bent double under the weight of stick men walking upright on their backs. In Church, as in society, women are unequal partners, the unseen, unheard servicers of men. Rather than challenging society's attitudes and prejudices, the Church embodies them, frequently acting as a block to the ideal of justice outlined above. Throughout history it has attempted theological and moral justification of sexual injustice. Scripture and Christian tradition have been used to maintain the inferior status of women in the Church, society, and the marriage relationship. And where this inferiority is not consciously affirmed, it is somehow perpetuated by the Church's language and selective memory.

So women remain invisible, their identity and experience of scant interest and little importance.

Women's Work in the Church

The Church has been an active participant in the debate about the nature and function of work. But it cannot be an effective commentator on work without reflecting on its own position as a provider of work. It must consider what opportunities there are for service in the Church, and what priorities it gives to the work there is to be done. Where it employs workers, how well does it pay them? The Church should surely be the last institution to be exploiting people by capitalising on their goodwill and commitment. How does the paid and unpaid work provided by the Church enable the use and development of people's gifts? Is there adequate training, support and recognition for the work that is done? Is the more fulfilling work available to people regardless of their sex? Is the necessary but monotonous work fairly distributed?

The Martha Myth

Unfortunately the employment position of women is frequently mirrored in their position as workers in the Church. What more effective illustration of occupational segregation could there be than a Church where men preside at lectern and altar and women reside in the pews or work behind the scenes? This is the impression that many people have of women's participation in Church life, and not without good reason. Fortunately, it is not the whole picture. The General Synod Standing Committee on 'The Community of Women and Men in the Church'[1] undertook a survey of the participation of women in the Church at parochial, deanery and diocesan levels, and found an enormous variety of practice. For them it soon emerged that

> the 'Martha myth'—the description of women as inarticulate pew fodder, compulsive cleaners of brass and typically brewers of tea—is in urgent need of re-examination.[2]

The Church of England's employment policy is currently being examined. If a man and a woman, both of whom are candidates for full-time ministry in the Church, get married, both are likely to be seeking a title in a parish. But it is often suggested that the wife should be non-stipendiary or part-time. This has very serious implications for the woman as she may lose her pension rights.[3]

This re-examination needs to be done by Church congregations themselves. Unless they do so, they may remain unaware both of the contributions women are making and of the prejudices and blocks to their participation which undoubtedly do exist. There is a necessary distinction to

be made between common beliefs and expectations about the involvement of women and the actual facts. The Standing Committee identified the problem as,

to disentangle the roles women actually play in the structures of the Church from what roles they are expected to play and what roles they themselves expect to play.[4]

Asking the simplest questions raises awareness. For instance: what proportion of the congregation of which you are a member is made up of women? Who leads the worship, preaches, serves, leads house groups, cleans, visits, teaches in the Sunday School, launders and makes the tea? Who runs the crèche? Who makes the decisions on behalf of whom? Maybe your Parochial Church Council has more women on it than men. Who talks most? What happens further up in the church hierarchy—on deanery, diocesan and national synods and boards? Where are the imbalances? Are they really a reflection of the abilities among churchpeople? Can we see a vision of the Church as a community of mutual stewardship and service, over against the exploitative and unequal patterns of the 'secular' world? Can the Church learn to long for the full contribution of women rather than fearing and fighting it?

How can the Church Serve Women?

Firstly, the Church can recognise, encourage and benefit from the diverse experiences, abilities, hopes, and ways of self-expression among women. In so doing, it will question the common elevation of sex-stereotyping behaviour as the only model of a Christian life-style. It would also challenge assumptions about what constitutes 'real' family life and 'true' relationships. The popular perception of the family, for example, is of a secure, conflict-free haven somehow immune to outside turbulence. That is not the way most people in families experience family life. Experience tells us that it can be a bed of nails as well as of roses. For women especially, home is also a place of work. The symbol of family life can be a useful one but only if it reflects reality, the upheavals, risks and necessary adjustments which are part of every family's experience.

What can the Church Learn from Women?

In order to serve women, the Church has to listen and learn. A vital first step would be to train and encourage spokeswomen, and to make sure that all committees and Church bodies—and not just local Church councils—include significant numbers of women. Such an 'equal opportunity' policy would require positive discrimination and effort. Here is a challenge to the Church to recognise that women's contributions are worth having and that much can be learned from them. This is not a lone cry in the wilderness. The authors of the General Synod Standing Committee report say:

> if the Church is serious in its concern that women as well as men be appointed to senior positions then the Church ... will have to pursue a policy of seeking out women candidates ... the Group therefore see some positive advantage in suggesting that ... some definitive guidelines of representation of women and men in Boards and Councils be set down.[5]

God the Disturber

To some people, this may be highly disturbing. So the image of God as Disturber is particularly pertinent, and there is ample biblical material with which to undergird and development this notion. In the midst of all the change and disruption, there is God, in the very midst, working out the divine purpose for humanity. The concept is a challenging one, but also comforting. It witnesses to a God who is present and actively engaged in the world. Security is not to be found in the absence of change, but rather in the midst of it. Far from being a lamentable sign of decay, disturbance can be a positive, God-given opportunity for re-evaluation, for the creation of a new order, which faith believes can emerge out of chaos.

With such a vision of God, the Church can face up to change with courage and excitement. But what about its own self understanding?

A New Image

The image of the Church as an exclusive, immoveable stronghold, the full source of security in a rapidly changing world, becomes no longer adequate. Now a new image seeks to burst through, expressing the energising and disturbing force of the Church, young, vital, exciting! New Testament ideas of 'the salt of the earth' and 'the leaven in the lump' may be helpful, or even of 'the vine' which, having found its way into everything, gets all knotted up, and then cannot extricate itself! Perhaps the most helpful idea is that of 'the wilderness Church', its history rooted in uncertainty and insecurity. Nudged by a disturbing God, the wilderness Church leaves the things behind which gave it security but also held it captive, and ventures out into the unknown. This is a repentant and humble community, it lives without immediate certainties. Ever moving forward on its pilgrimage, it has by no means arrived, may not know 'where it is at', and is unsure of exactly where it is going. But it is moving on.

Facing Change

A Church that can encourage people to face change is perhaps our most urgent need. But within the body of Christ a wealth of experience and resource exists, to help us on our way. Women have experience of coping with some of the most urgent issues confronting Church and society today. It is they who have learned how. Constant calls are made on women's powers of adaptation over their life cycle. In meeting the fluctuating demands of growing families they have had to develop flexibility, weigh up priorities and make compromises. Their attachment to the labour market has been more tenuous because of family obligations. In order to cope with this they were seeking alternative employment patterns long before male unemployment reached the severe proportions at which it now stands, and the shortage of employment prompted experiment in job sharing and the like. Continuous full-time employment is still considered important for career advancement, and people are still assessed by what they do rather than by who they are. Women have had to derive their identity and self-respect from within rather than from external job circumstances. They can lead the way in creating a concept of personhood which is not based on a person's waged occupation.

Most significantly, women have been experimenting with alternative ways of organising. The Women's Movement is not the first to espouse the principle of co-operation over competition, but it is perhaps the most visible challenge at present to the rigid competitive and hierarchical structures which govern our society.

They have been developing ways of working and relating in which one person's needs are seen to be as important as another's, and in which process is as important as end result.

Service and Co-operation

It can be argued that service and co-operation are the organising principles of women's lives and that it is these principles which society needs to adopt if it is to become more just and caring. The qualities which all people possess, but which are perhaps most highly developed in women, are the ones we need for social advance.

Competition, individualism and other traits commonly thought to be characteristic of male identity will only take us so far.

And we need to embark on a new path. The new path will be one which redresses the balance with those 'female qualities'. Since this path has rarely been trodden before, we cannot be sure where it will lead. We have no option but to try it.

SYNOPSIS

Part One of this report surveys a wide range of experience that women have of work, both paid and unpaid. The intention is to put the record straight. For a start, it is often not realised that women's participation in the labour market is no recent phenomenon. For over a century women have constituted nearly one-third of the total British labour force, rising to over 40 per cent by the 1980s. The 1984 Department of Employment's Women and Employment Survey concluded that trends indicate an increase in the number of women expecting to spend their adult years in the labour market, much of that time being employed in part time jobs.

Despite the overwhelming evidence that women seek jobs for much the same reasons as men—money, status, fulfilment and companionship—their employment is still considered to be of secondary importance to that of men. Old attitudes and stereotypes may be gradually breaking down, but they still persist strongly enough to mean that women's work is generally characterised by lower pay and status.

Women are often still expected to be 'two-shift' workers. Having finished their paid work, there is the unpaid work at home to do. This affects participation in trade union activities, for example, because attendance at union meetings is so hard to fit in. What is needed is positive action—seeking to make possible the equal opportunities that legislation is intended to encourage and enable.

Women's unemployment is a problem which is often underestimated and unrecognised. The myth is that all a woman really wants is a husband, home and children! Sadly, in the absence of meaningful alternatives, many women seem to opt prematurely for marriage and motherhood.

CHAPTER
THREE

The primary sphere in which women are expected to operate—even those in full-time jobs—is the home. Housework is seen as the major occupation of women, but there is little recognition of the contribution which housework makes to social and economic production and the general well-being and functioning of society.

The quiet, unseen caring for relatives, young and old, falls largely on women. It is home-based, often requiring considerable personal sacrifice on the part of the carer; it is financially and emotionally costly, and has often to be borne in isolation and without support.

CHAPTER
FOUR

The context in which this sexual division of labour has evolved has been two hundred years of industrialisation, with massive shifts of population to the towns, and gradual geographical separation of home and workplace. All this has led to the defining of two distinct spheres—public and private, workplace and home, wages and unwaged, his and hers. Thus women's aspirations, abilities and contributions to society have become focused on their role as mother and homemaker.

CHAPTER FIVE

In Part Two, the convictions underlying this report are made explicit. We argue that the task of reflecting upon and learning about God and human experience can never be said to be complete. Theology is not a package from which can be deduced eternal truths, to determine human behaviour regardless of culture or generation. It is, rather, an exciting, challenging and sometimes threatening dialogue between God and human beings. It must inevitably take into account new discoveries or emphases with each generation. One such discovery is that the world is not necessarily seen by women in the same way as men have always portrayed it. Women are finding a voice—and the Church, along with everyone else, must choose whether to listen to or ignore it.

CHAPTER
SIX

Justice is a profoundly important theme in the Old and New Testaments and throughout the Christian tradition. But, so long as men continue to do the lion's share of defining, shaping and controlling society, justice is threatened. The attitude of Jesus to women contrasted powerfully with that of his contemporaries. The coming reign of God, already present and active in Jesus, includes and endorses women as equal partners in the human vocation to serve and shape the world for God and good.

CHAPTER
SEVEN
How such justice can be brought about is the crucial question. Women's experience has much to contribute here, and the themes of Stewardship and Servanthood shed helpful light.

Stewardship extends far beyond its traditional application to possessions, time and talents. We need to think of it in terms of the proper care of dependents, the education of our children and the meeting of common human needs. In this sense it is mainly women who have been stewards.

In terms of servanthood—also an apt word to describe women's role—a distinction needs drawing between service, freely chosen in response to God's call, and subservience. The latter is not a Christian virtue.

CHAPTER
EIGHT
All this has implications for the Church. What more effective illustration of occupational segregation could there be than a Church where men preside at lectern and altar and women reside in pews or work behind the scenes? Fortunately this stereotype does not tell the whole story. Important and exciting changes are afoot.

Many people may find this disturbing. But God as Disturber is a powerful biblical image, calling for a faith which believes that a new order can emerge out of chaos. With a God like this, change can be faced confidently.

REFERENCES

Chapter One

[1] *R.S.V. Bible:* Genesis 1.27, 28
[2] Ann Oakley: *Subject Women,* Fontana Paperbacks 1981, pp. 145–7.
[3] Ibid. p.147.
[4] Martin & Roberts: *Women and Employment. A Lifetime Perspective,* Dept. of Employment, OPCS, 1984, p.11.
[5] Ibid. p.187.
[6] University of Warwick Institute for Employment Research: *Women's working lives; evidence from the National Training Survey,* 1982, pp. 107, 111.
[7] Sanders & Reed: *Kitchen Sink or Swim,* Penguin Books 1982, p.82.
[8] Ibid. p.82.
[9] *The Guardian:* 13.6.84.
[10] Centre for Research on European Women; *CREW Report,* Vol. IV, No. 6.
[11] Op. cit. Martin & Roberts, p.77.

Chapter Two

[1] Op. cit. Martin & Roberts, p.33.
[2] Ibid. p.33.
[3] Department of Education and Science. Statistics of Teachers in Service in England and Wales, 1983 Table B 129.
[4] Op. cit. Sanders & Reed, p.80.
[5] Equal Opportunities Commission: *Do You Provide Equal Opportunities?* Revised edition 1985, pp. 13,14.
[6] Department of Education and Science Statistical Bulletin: *Enrolments on non-advanced courses of further education,* April 1984.
[7] TUC Report: *Women in the Labour Market,* 1983, p. 17.
[8] Dept. of Employment, HMSO: *New Earnings Survey,* Part A October 1985, pp. 78, 59, 58, 51.
[9] Equal Opportunities Commission: *New Earnings Survey Statistical Guide. Men and Women,* p.89.
[10] *Wages Councils: A Submission to Government.* BSR Industrial Committee WP 19, August 1985, p. 11.
[11] *Back to the Sweatshops—Wages Councils Proposals,* Low Pay Unit pamphlet No. 37, 1985.
[12] *The Guardian:* 26.6.85.
[13] Finer Joint Action Committee: Report of the Committee on One Parent Families Vol. 1, HMSO 1974, p. 255.
[14] Brown & Madge: *Despite the Welfare State. A report on the SSRC/DHSS programme of research into transmitted deprivation,* London Heinemann Educational Books, 1982, p.45.
[15] Ursula Huws: *The New Homeworkers,* LPU No. 28, 1984, p.52.

[16] Liz Bisset and Ursula Huws: *Sweated Labour—homeworking in Britain today,* LPU No. 33, 1985.

[17] Paul Harrison: *Inside the Inner City,* Pelican Books, 1985, p.65.

[18] *The Guardian:* 2.9.85.

[19] Eaton & Gill: *Trade Union Directory,* Pluto Press, 1983 (2nd edition), p. 210.

[20] Colin Brown: *P.S.I. Black & White Britain, Heinemann Educational Books, 1984, pp. 150, 151.*

[21] *Unemployment Unit Briefing Statistical Supplement, August 1985.*

[22] Op. cit. EOC: *Men and Women,* p.78.

[23] Beatrix Campbell: *Wigan Pier Revisited,* Virago Press, 1984, p.65.

[24] *The Guardian,* 9.10.84.

Chapter Three

[1] Ann Oakley: *Housewife,* Penguin Books, 1976, p.6.

[2] Ibid. p.99.

[3] Janet Finch: *Married to the Job,* George Allen & Unwin, 1983.

[4] Ibid. p.78.

[5] Chris Beales: *Work? You Must be Joking,* in *Respond!,* Tees-side Industrial Mission, 1984, p.3.

[6] Anna Briggs: *Who Cares?* Report of a door to door survey into the numbers of people caring for dependent relatives, published by the Association of Carers, June 1983, p. 12.

[7] Equal Opportunities Commission: *Caring for the elderly and handicapped; community care policies and women's lives,* p.17.

[8] Jeanette Longfield: *Ask the Family,* NCVO, p.6.

[9] Equal Opportunities Commission: *I want to work, but what about the kids?* p.7.

[10] A. Norris: *Survey of Childcare at Freemans,* Unpublished.

[11] Dept. of Employment Survey, p.39.

Chapter Four

[1] Margaret Mead: *Male and Female,* Pelican Books, 1962, p.12.

[2] Jean Baker Miller: *Towards a New Psychology of Women,* Pelican Books, 1978, p.78.

Chapter Six

[1] Mary Evans: *Women in the Bible,* Paternoster Press, p.45.

[2] *C.E.B.* Cranfield: *Mark,* C.U.P., 1959, p.463 (quoted by Mary Evans).

[3] Op. cit. Mary Evans, p.52.

Chapter Seven

[1] Janet Radcliffe Richards: *The Sceptical Feminist,* Pelican Books, 1982, p.211.

[2] Op. cit. Jean Baker Miller, p.43.

[3] Op. cit. Janet Radcliffe Richards, p.217.

Chapter Eight

[1] Dr M. Hewitt (Chair.): *Community of Men and Women in the Church,* General Synod Working Party Report No. 15, SC8515, 5.3.85. Published February 1986 as *'Servants of the Lord'.*

[2] Ibid. p.75.

[3] See A.C.C.M. Occasional Paper No. 16 *Joint Ministries Consultation,* ACCM, 1984. *Joint-Ministry: A Practical Guide,* ACCM, Spring 1986.

[4] Op. cit. Dr M. Hewitt, p.77.

[5] Ibid. p.81.

BIBLIOGRAPHY

Jeanette Longfield: *Ask the Family:* Shattering the Myths about Family Life. Bedford Square Press/NCVO 1984.

Jean Baker Miller: *Towards a New Psychology of Women.* Pelican 1978.

Jo Morris: *No More Peanuts:* An Evaluation of Women's Work. NCCL 1983.

Ann Oakley: *Subject Women.* Fontana 1981.

Rosemary Radford Reuther: *Sexism and God-Talk:* towards a feminist theology. SCM 1983.

Janet Radcliffe Richards: *The Sceptical Feminist.* Pelican 1982.

Elaine Storkey: *What's Right with Feminism?* Third Way Books. SPCK 1985.

Amrit Wilson: *Finding a Voice:* Asian Women in Britain. Virago 1978.

The Changing Experience of Women: Open University set book. Blackwell 1982.

Women in the Labour Market: A TUC Report. TUC 1983.

Women in Top Jobs. Policy Studies Institute 1979.

MEMBERS OF THE WORKING GROUP

Rosemary Dawson (author)
Project Worker, Women and Employment Project, Manchester Diocesan Board for Social Responsibility/Girls Friendly Society.

Caroline Barker Bennett*†‡
Industrial Chaplain, Northumbrian Industrial Mission.

Alison Norris
Industrial Chaplain, South London Industrial Mission.

Alison Webster
Secretary, Social Policy Committee of the Board for Social Responsibility.

Chris Beales (secretary)
Secretary, Industrial and Economic Affairs Committee of the Board for Social Responsibility.

(This symbol* indicates a member of the Industrial and Economic Affairs Committee, † a member of the Board for Social Responsibility, and ‡ a member of the General Synod.)

All the above have acted in a private capacity and not as representatives of the organisations mentioned. The views expressed are those of the Working Group, or of the authors named, as applicable. They should not necessarily be thought to represent the opinions of anyone else.

FOR FURTHER READING

All reports and Working Papers from the Industrial and Economic Affairs Committee are available from Church House Bookshop, Great Smith Street, London SW1P 3BU.

Reports

Growth, Justice and Work. July 1985. 50 pages. CIO Publishing. £2.50.
Five essays whose writers are convinced that Christian insights impinge urgently upon economic policies and political programmes.
Perspectives on Economics. September 1984. 82 pages. CIO Publishing. £2.50.
Reflections on aspects of the changing British economic system in the context of Christian theology.
Transnational Corporations: Confronting the Issues. April 1983. 80 pages. CIO Publishing. £2.20.
Seven essays concentrating on the nature of the impact of TNCs in the third world and the problems caused for organised labour in the developed countries.
Winters of Discontent: Industrial Conflict—A Christian Perspective. May 1981. 60 pages. CIO Publishing. £1.75.
A study of industrial conflict examining the characteristics of industrial society and industry's main groupings.
Work and the Future: Technology, World Development and Jobs in the Eighties. November 1979. 44 pages. CIO Publishing. £1.
An analysis of the experience of work and the impact of new technology, together with a moral perspective and the need for experiment with new forms of organisation.